The Causal
and
The Casual in History

T0345973

The Causal

and

The Casual in History

by

JOHN BUCHAN

M.A., LL.D., M.P.

THE REDE LECTURE

1929

CAMBRIDGE

AT THE UNIVERSITY PRESS

1929

CAMBRIDGE
UNIVERSITY PRESS

University Printing House, Cambridge CB2 8BS, United Kingdom

Published in the United States of America by Cambridge University Press, New York

Cambridge University Press is part of the University of Cambridge.

It furthers the University's mission by disseminating knowledge in the pursuit of education, learning and research at the highest international levels of excellence.

www.cambridge.org
Information on this title: www.cambridge.org/9781107698222

© Cambridge University Press 1929

First published 1929
First paperback edition 2014

A catalogue record for this publication is available from the British Library

ISBN 978-1-107-69822-2 Paperback

THE CAUSAL
AND
THE CASUAL IN HISTORY

Mr Vice-Chancellor,
Ladies and Gentlemen

A VISITOR TO CAMBRIDGE FROM THE
sister University, especially a visitor
on such an errand as mine, is not likely to
be forgetful of the special genius of the
place. He remembers that for some centuries Cambridge has been the chosen
home of the natural sciences; that, while
keeping a shrewd eye upon practical appli-
cations, she has not allowed the lure of
immediate rewards to divert her from the
quest of truth; and that one of her tradi-
tional toasts has been "God bless the higher
mathematics and may they never be of the

5

slightest use to anybody". Here, if any-where on the globe, he may expect to find a proper notion of what constitutes a science. He will also, if he have historical interests, remember that within recent years Cambridge has been fruitful in pronounce-ments on the meaning of history. In 1903 Professor Bury proclaimed: "History is a science—no less and no more"; while it has been the happy task of your present Regius Professor to emphasise the other side of the truth—that Clio is a Muse, the daughter of Zeus and Mnemosyne, and the mother of Orpheus.

I propose, with Cambridge's scientific fame in my mind, and with these sayings of two of her most eminent historians to guide me, to make some further observa-tions on the Muse of History. She is a lady of many parts. She has her laboratory, no doubt, and her record office; she has, beyond question, her lyre and her singing robes. But the character in which I would exhibit her this afternoon is homelier than these. I can picture Clio with knitted brows, striving to disentangle the why and the wherefore of things. I can picture her with rapt eyes, making epic and drama out of the past. But I can picture her most easily with the puzzled and curious face of a child, staring at the kaleidoscope of the centuries, and laughing—yes, laughing—at an inconsequence that defies logic, and whimsicalities too fantastic for art.

I

Let me begin by making concessions to every school. History is an art, and it is also a science; we may say that it is an art which is always trying to become more of a science. As a science it is concerned with causation. The past, if it is to satisfy intelligent minds, must be presented as a sequence of effects and causes. History is not content with an accumulation of facts; it seeks to establish relations between facts. Like every other science, it is a form of thought, and, like every other science, it

7

aims at the attainment of truth. The past cannot be regarded as a mere pageant. Events do not follow each other only in succession of time. Even from the point of view of art, history must have its own inevitableness; and, from the point of view of science, it must aim at representing the whole complex of the past as a chain, each link riveted to the other by a causal necessity.

That is an ideal which we may well admire. It represents an instinct at which we dare not cavil—one of the oldest of human instincts, the instinct to rationalise. I learn from the newspapers that there is a hopeful movement on foot to-day towards what is called the "rationalising" of industry, and there is no reason why the modest labours of Clio's domain should be exempt from the impulse. History must be more than a chronicle; it must be synoptic and interpretative.

In practice, rationalisation may take many forms. To begin with, there are the high philosophers, the professional meta-physicians. If Bolingbroke was right, and history is philosophy teaching by examples, it is clearly most important to get at the philosophy. Then there are those who fix their eyes upon scientific method, and, like Taine, believe that by means of a number of categories of determinable causes every historical event can be mathematically explained. Others are content to seek a formula, and there are many kinds of formulas. There is the formula derived from metaphysics—the Hegelian dialectic, for example, with its sequence of thesis and antithesis and synthesis; or, in a simpler form, Louis Blanc's succession of authority, individualism and fraternity; or, simpler still, the mysticism which finds the key in a single aspect, like Karl Marx's economic interpretation. Or you may have the unifying notion in the shape of a metaphor, a pictorial conception, such as the idea of the past as a cyclic or a spiral process. You may get a loose interpretative principle in

2

something akin to biological evolution, or you may find it in an ethical or theological purpose. Lord Acton saw in history the working of the moral law, and Bishop Stubbs the revelation of the "Almighty Ruler of the world" busied with "leading the world on to the better, but never forcing, and out of the evil of man's working bringing continually that which is good".

There is no word to be said against the ambition of philosophers and scientists and even theologians to bring light and order into the dark places of the past. Every historian must have a thesis, some principle of illumination to guide him, and the value of his work will largely depend upon the sanity and profundity of that thesis. But I would suggest that, the subject-matter of history being what it is, we should be chary of becoming too dogmatic about any principle of interpretation which we put forward. For history works under conditions wholly unlike those of the natural sciences, and historic truth must be something very different from mathematical truth, or even from biological truth.

The philosophers need not trouble us. The awful gambols of a metaphysical doctrine are apt now and then to make nonsense of history, as when Hegel contemplated the stately process of the Absolute Will, and found its final expression in Germany before 1840—a view more flattering to Germany than to the Absolute Will. But if the metaphysician likes to explain everything by some such process, he is welcome to try, so long as he admits that he cannot expound its precise working.

The scientific historian is more dangerous. The older school, of the type of Buckle and Guizot, believed that they had established historical laws of universal validity, and provided a clockwork uniformity of effects and causes. It would appear that they misunderstood the kind of material with which they had to deal. M. Bergson has shown us that half the blunders of philosophy are due to the application of the methods and ideals of physical science to spheres of thought where they are strictly inapplicable. In the kaleidoscope of the past we cannot, as a rule, sort out effects and causes with any precision, nor can we weigh events in the meticulous scales which science demands. Even when causes are reasonably plain, their classification eludes us. We cannot tell which is the *causa causans*, which are proximate, or efficient, or final. We must be content with generalisations which are only generalisations and not laws, with broad effects and massed colours. The weakness of the scientific historian is that he underrates the complexity of human nature. He would turn mankind into automata, motives into a few elementary emotions, and the infinitely varied web of life into a simple geometrical pattern. Order and simplicity are great things, but they must be natural to the subject and not due to the blindness of the historian. You remember Sainte-Beuve's comment on Guizot:

I am one of those who doubt if it is given to man to embrace the causes and sources of his history with this completeness and certitude. It is as much as he can do to reach an imperfect understanding of the present....History seen from a distance undergoes a strange metamorphosis; it produces the illusion—most dangerous of all—that it is rational. The perversities, the follies, the ambitions, the thousand queer accidents which compose it, all these disappear. Every accident becomes a necessity....Such history is far too logical to be true.

On this point we are perhaps a little more modest to-day than our fathers were. But we are always apt to forget that history cannot give us the precise and continuous causal connections which we look for in the physical sciences. All that we get are a number of causal suggestions, with a good many gaps in them, and if we try to get more we shall do violence to historical truth. We shall be in danger of writing history in order to prove something, and thereby losing that "disinterested intellectual curiosity" which is the only avenue to truth. We shall try to make the accidental the inevitable, and to explain the inexplicable. We shall refuse to recognise the fundamental irrationality of a large part of Clio's domain.

An example of this fallacy is the attitude of the would-be scientific historian towards great men. The hero in history is a terrible nuisance to the lover of dapper generalities. He breaks the symmetry and spoils the syllogism. What is to be done with him? The scientific mind likes to deal with human nature in the lump, for it is aware that you can generalise with reasonable accuracy about the behaviour of masses of people, when you cannot dogmatise about any single one of them. But what about the daimonic figures who obstinately refuse to be merged in the mass? The embarrassed scientist is driven to one of two courses. Either he declares that the great people had but little influence on the course of events, that the real motive force was this or that intellectual movement or economic grouping. But in many cases this is simply

not the truth. The great individuals—
Alexander, Caesar, Mahomet, Charle-
magne, Luther, Calvin, Peter the Great,
Napoleon, Lenin—cannot be explained in
the terms of any contemporary movement.
They are in a sense the children of their
age, but they bring to their age more than
they draw from it; they seem to be, like
Melchizedek, without recognisable an-
cestry, and by the sheer force of personality
and mind they switch the world into a new
orbit.... Or he will try to submerge them in
the mass by arguing that they were not so
great after all. This necessity may partly
account for the sansculottism of a certain
type of historian, who is always attempting
to deflate the majestic reputations of history, and to reduce the great figures of the
past to a drab level of mediocrity. Partly,
no doubt, these essays in belittlement are
the result of what is called in the jargon
of to-day an "inferiority complex", the
jealousy of small minds perturbed by
the spectacle of something beyond their

compass. They see a chance of winning an easy notoriety. An old Cambridge friend of mine had a simile for such people; he said that they were like some Greek of the decadence who broke the nose of an Apollo of Pheidias in order to make the Goths laugh. But, for the honour of human nature, I like to think it is partly the desire of the embarrassed scientist to have less truculent material to work with. Once again, the trouble is that the result is not the truth. Such denigratory efforts may explain many things in a great man, but not his greatness.

The fault, of course, is that of undue simplification. It is the application by a false analogy of the ideals and methods of certain physical sciences to a domain where they are not relevant. In physics we reduce a complex to the operations of constant and measurable forces, but no such mechanical simplification is possible with the inconstants of human history. The movement of mankind is not by a single-gauge track; there is a network of tracks, and the one actually taken may owe its choice to the blindest chance. Rationalise the facts as much as you please—and you can often carry the process a long way—there will remain things which you cannot rationalise, things which you can only call accidents, and which cannot be explained by any logical terms. Instead of the causal we find the casual. I do not for one moment argue that these incomprehensible factors are incapable of rationalisation by some higher intelligence than our own; I only say that we cannot fit them into any mortal scheme of effects and causes. The President of the Immortals has not chosen to take us into his confidence.

Explanation and interpretation, let me repeat, are the essence of history. An historical event can be partially explained by many causes, but there may be some little thing without which it could not have happened, and that little thing may come out of the void, without any apparent justification for its existence. Nevertheless, but for it the history of a decade or a century would have gone differently. Everywhere in the record of the past we find those sparks which fire the powder mines, and in the absence of which the powder might have become useless and never have exploded at all. Let us be a little chary about accepting the so-called "streams of inevitable tendency" which are the delight in each generation of simple souls, and give them the opportunity of posing as minor prophets and announcing the "decline of the West" or the "recrudescence of barbarism", or some such journalistic slogan. The historian is wise if, like the Romans of the early Empire, he admits Fortuna and even Sors to a place in his Pantheon, and concedes the eternal presence of the irrational and the inexplicable.

It is a recognition which encourages intellectual humility. I venture to think, too, that our sense of the mystery and variousness of life is enlarged, when we realise that the very great may spring from the very small. How does Edmund Burke put it? "A common soldier, a child, a girl at the door of an inn, have changed the face of fortune, and almost of Nature". History is full of these momentous trifles—the accident which kills or preserves in life some figure of destiny; the weather on some critical battlefield, like the fog at Lützen or the snow at Towton; the change of wind which brings two fleets to a decisive action; the severe winter of 1788 which produces the famine of 1789, and thereby perhaps the French Revolution; the birth or the death of a child; a sudden idea which results in some potent invention. Let me give you an instance from the most recent history. The success of Turkish Nationalism under Kemal was due to the complete rout of the Greek armies in 1922 in Asia Minor. That ill-omened Greek campaign was largely due to the restoration in 1920 of King Constantine, which led to the Western Allies dissociating themselves from Greek policy and leaving Greece to her own devices. King Constantine was recalled as a consequence of a general election when M. Venizelos was defeated, and that election was held because young King Alexander, the *protégé* of the Allies, died early in the autumn of 1920. The cause of his death was blood-poisoning due to the bite of a pet monkey in the palace gardens. I cannot better Mr Churchill's comment: "A quarter of a million persons died of that monkey's bite".

To look for such pregnant trifles is an instructive game, very suitable for academic circles in the winter season. But it must be played according to the rules. The business is to find the momentous accident, and obviously the smaller you make the accident, the more you reduce it to its ultimate elements, the more startling will be the disproportion between the vast consequence and the minute cause. The accident must be small, and it must be a true parent of consequences. Not every one will serve our purpose. Take Pascal's query—as to what would have happened to the world had Cleopatra's nose been a little shorter? The answer, I think, is—Not very much. Egypt, as the granary of the Roman world, was obviously a trump card for ambition to seize, and its importance did not depend upon the profile of its queen. Take another familiar speculation—what difference would it have made if Clive's pistol had not missed fire when, as a young man, he attempted suicide? Again, I think, the right answer is—Not a great deal. India was ripe for British conquest; if Clive had not led the way, some other would. In the middle decades of the sixteenth century a great deal seemed to depend upon the appearance of royal heirs, and historians have speculated as to what would have happened if Anne Boleyn had borne a male child, or Mary Tudor, or Mary of Scotland when she was the wife of the Dauphin of France. I doubt if there would have been any substantial change. The main lines of the future had been already determined by the complex of economic and intellectual forces which were responsible for the Reformation.

But let me offer to you—in the spirit of the game which I have suggested—one or two cases where destiny does seem for one moment to have trembled in the balance.

II

The first is a November day in London in the year 1612. There is a curious hush in the city. Men and women go about with soft feet and grave faces. People whisper anxiously at street corners; even the noise in the taverns is stilled. The only sound is a melancholy wind howling up the river. Suddenly above the wind rises the tolling of a bell, and at the sound women cover their heads and weep, and men uncover theirs and pray. For it is the Great Bell of Paul's, which tolls only for a royal death. It means that Henry, Prince of Wales, at the age of eighteen is dead.......He died of a malignant fever which puzzled the doctors. It was an age of strange diseases, but a prince was jealously guarded against them, and I think he must have caught the infection on one of his visits to Sir Walter Raleigh in the Bloody Tower, when he went to talk of high politics and hear tales of the Indies, and admire the model ship called *The Prince*, which Raleigh and Keymis had made for him. Prisons in those days, even prisons reserved for grandees, were haunts of pestilence, and in some alley of the Tower, in that heavy autumn weather, he may have caught the germ which brought him to his death. A chance breath drew the malignant micro-organism into his body, and he was doomed.

Supposing that breath had not been drawn, and the Prince had lived the full span of life, for there was uncommon tenacity in his stock. So far as we can judge, he resembled his sister, Elizabeth of the Palatine, who was for many years the star to adventurous youth. In no respect did he resemble his brother Charles. He was a *revenant* from the Elizabethan Age, and his chief mentor was Walter Raleigh himself. He was a Protestant enthusiast, to whom Protestantism was identified with patriotism, after the stalwart fashion of Cromwell thirty years later. Not for him any philandering with Spain. He would have gladly warned England as Cromwell did in 1656: "Truly your great enemy is the Spaniard! He is naturally so—by reason of that enmity which is in him against whatsoever is of God". When a French marriage was proposed to him he told his father that "he was resolved that two religions should not lie in his bed".

Had Henry lived, what might have happened? In European politics he would have made Britain the leader of the struggle against the Counter-Reformation. We cannot assess his abilities in the field, but, judging from the respect in which Raleigh held his brains, it is possible that he might have taken the place of Gustavus Adolphus. In any case Britain was

24

a greater power than Sweden, and almost certainly he would have led the Continental Protestants. As for domestic affairs, it is clear that he had that indefinable magnetism which his sister had, and which attracted easily and instantly a universal popularity. He would have been a people's king. More, he would have shared the politics of the vast bulk of his subjects, their uncompromising Protestantism, their nascent imperialism. In ecclesiastical matters he would have found the *via media* which Charles missed. He would not have quarrelled with his Parliaments, for his views were theirs. They would have followed him voluntarily and raised no question of rights against the Crown, because the Crown thought as they did, and one does not question the rights of a willingly accepted leader. The change from the Tudor to the modern monarchy would have been of a very different kind. There would have been no Civil War. Cromwell might have died the first general in Europe and Duke of

25   4

Huntingdon, while the guide of the monarchy into new constitutional paths might have been a great Scotsman, James Graham, the first Duke of Montrose, who sometime about the year 1645 effected the union of the Scottish and English Parliaments.

Let us slip a hundred years and take the summer of 1711, when Marlborough was facing Villars before the famous *Ne Plus Ultra* line of trenches. His famous victories were behind him, and the campaign of that summer is not familiar to the world like the campaigns of Blenheim and Ramillies and Malplaquet. Yet I think the most wonderful of all the great Duke's exploits fell in that year, when he outwitted Villars and planted himself beyond the Scheldt at Oisy, between Villars and France, and within easy reach of Arras and Cambrai. Had he had his country behind him, I cannot but believe that he was in a position to take Paris and bring the French monarchy to its knees. But, as all the world knows, his country was not behind him. He had lost the Queen's favour. Some small thing—an increasing arrogance in the manners of the Duchess Sarah, an extra adroitness in the diplomacy of Mrs Masham —had wrought the change. Marlborough saw his triumphant career in the field cut short, and two years later came the Peace of Utrecht.

What might have happened had Mrs Masham been less persuasive and the Duchess Sarah less domineering? As I have said, I do not think that anything could have kept Paris from Marlborough. With its capture would have come the degradation of the French monarchy, and the downfall from his pedestal of the Grand Monarque. With such a cataclysm there was bound to be a complete revision of the French system of government. There would also have come one of those stirrings of national pride which have always made France one of the most formidable nations in the world, and, I think, a rallying of her people to some sort of national and popular kingship. After that? Well, there would have been no French Revolution, for there would have been no need for it. But something akin to the French Revolution was inevitable somewhere in Europe towards the close of the eighteenth century, for it was the only way to get rid of a certain amount of mediaeval lumber. Where would it have taken place? Possibly in Britain. It was fortunate, perhaps, that in the intrigues of Queen Anne's bedchamber, Mrs Masham got the better of the Duchess Sarah.

My next scene is in the last year of the century. I pass with some reluctance over the intervening years, for they include many critical hours. In particular there was that hour some time during a December night in the year 1745, in the town of Derby, when it was decided that Prince Charles should not march on London, but should retreat with his Highland army across the Border. Had the decision been otherwise, the Rebellion of the Forty-five might have succeeded, and much in British history might have been different. But I pass to a greater issue than the dynastic settlement of Britain—the French Revolution and the career of Napoleon. Professor Trevelyan, in a delightful essay, has expounded what might have been the course of history had Napoleon won the battle of Waterloo. That is not quite the kind of case we are in quest of, for the loss or winning of Waterloo was not a small thing. Let us go further back in Napoleon's career, to a day when the issue was not less momentous and the balance hung on a hair—the 19th day of Brumaire—the 9th day of November in the year 1799. The Government of the Directory was rotten; France was ripe for a change, for any policy or any leader that would give her what, after the first day or two, every revolution yearns for, order and peace. Napoleon, with his dubious Egyptian laurels fresh upon him, had arrived in Paris. The plot had been hatched and the conspirators assembled. The two Councils, the Council of the Ancients and the Council of the Five Hundred, had been summoned on that day, the 19th day of Brumaire, to meet at Saint-Cloud, and Sieyès and Napoleon had decided that by these assemblies the new Consulate should be formally authorised.

It is never wise to protract a *coup d'état*, and this one had been staged to occupy two days. On the afternoon of November 9th at Saint-Cloud, Napoleon was in a fever of impatience. His journey from Egypt, and the strain he had lately gone through, had caused an irritation in the skin of his sallow face, and now and then, in his excitement, he scratched it. He was a strange figure as he paced the little room facing on the park, while the Ancients assembled upstairs in the Salle Apollo, and the Five Hundred in the Orangerie below. At half-past three he made a silly, rambling speech to the Ancients, which none of them understood, and Bourrienne had to drag him away in the midst of general laughter. Then he proceeded to the Five Hundred, accompanied by a handful of grenadiers. He was shouted down, hustled about, and only extricated by his bodyguard. The game seemed irretrievably lost.......But in the meantime he had been scratching his inflamed face, and had caused it to bleed. Leaving his brother, Lucien, in the presidential chair to watch his interests, he went out of doors, and showed himself with his bleeding face to the soldiers. At once the rumour flew that there had been daggers used on the General, and that his life was in danger from loquacious civilians. It was enough. Presently Lucien joined him, and in a burning harangue to the troops made the most of that bleeding cheek. Murat, with a file of Guards, cleared out the Five Hundred, and, ere the November evening fell, Napoleon was not only the leader of the French Army, but the civilian head of the French people.

On one point among the wild events of that day all authorities are agreed. Napoleon fumbled and blundered, and the situation was saved by Lucien. But would Lucien have succeeded in his appeal to the troops but for the blood on his brother's face? It seems to me unlikely, as I read the story of that day. I am inclined to think that it was that fortunate affection of the skin, and the nervous excitement that caused him to scratch his face, which at a critical moment made plain Napoleon's path to the control of France.

Let us make another leap—to the hour of nine o'clock on the evening of May 2nd in the year 1863. The place is among the scrub and the rough meadows of that part of Virginia called the Wilderness, near the hamlet of Chancellorsville. General Hooker, "Fighting Joe Hooker", is in command of the Federal Army of the Potomac, which comprises something like 130,000 men. He is the last hope of the Government in

Washington, who have not been having much luck with their generals. He has promised them a crushing victory, and Lincoln, in the War Department there, is sitting anxiously at the end of the telegraph wire. Hooker has crossed the Rappahannock, and believes that the road is open before him to Richmond. In front of him lies a Confederate Army, the Army of Northern Virginia; it numbers not much more than 62,000 men, less than half the Federal force, but its commander is Robert Lee, and his chief lieutenant is Stonewall Jackson.

Hooker has followed a dangerous plan. He has divided his big army into two separate wings, thereby giving the small Confederate force the advantage of the interior lines. Jeb Stuart with his cavalry has given Lee prompt information about every Federal move.......Very early it became clear that Hooker intended to turn the Confederate left. Lee, with the audacity of supreme genius, decided that, on the contrary, he would turn the Federal right, and make the outflanker the outflanked. Secretly, silently, Jackson made his way through the thick bush and the swamps of the Wilderness forest, and by the late afternoon of May 2nd Hooker's right, utterly unsuspicious, suddenly became aware, by the rush of small deer and birds from the woods, that Jackson was upon them.......By seven o'clock the battle of Chancellorsville had been won. Hooker was in full retreat.......But in a rout strange things may happen. Detachments of the Federals straggled about in the darkness, and in the gloom of the woods came into conflict with Confederate detachments, and there was much wild firing. Jackson and his staff, galloping to direct the pursuit, ran into the 18th North Carolina regiment, and were taken for the enemy. The Carolinians fired a volley in the confusion, and Jackson fell with three bullets in him. Eight days later he died.

It was the blindest mischance, but it had

momentous consequences. In Jackson, Lee lost his right-hand and a third of his brains. Two months after Chancellorsville he fought the indecisive action of Gettysburg, an action in which the absence of complete victory meant defeat. Lee always said that if he had had Jackson with him he would have won the battle, and I believe that he was right. If Lee had won Gettysburg then I am convinced that there would have been a negotiated peace. The North was sick to death of the war, and a Southern victory in Pennsylvania would have broken the last remnant of Washington's nerve. Lincoln's stern determination to accept nothing less than complete victory and unconditional surrender would have been over-ruled.......What would have happened then? Lincoln would not have been assassinated; there would have been little bitterness left over on either side, since neither was the conqueror. In the inevitable reconstruction which must have followed it is difficult to believe that two such men as Lincoln and Lee would not have achieved a reasonable compromise, and a reconstituted United States. There must have been drastic, and probably beneficial, changes in that most cumbrous instrument, the American constitution. Slavery would have been abolished on equitable terms, for Lee was at least as eager in that cause as Lincoln. Beyond that we need not penetrate. But we can at least say that America's development, economic, political, constitutional and spiritual, would have been very different from what it is to-day. That North Carolina volley, fired blindly in the woodland dusk on that May evening, was one of the most fateful in history.

Half a century more and we come to the Great War. I suppose we must rank the First Battle of the Marne as one of the two or three decisive battles of the world. If Germany had won, she would have attained the victory of which she dreamed "before the leaves fell". What was the *causa causans*, the little extra weighting of the scales, which turned the balance on that long battle front between the suburbs of Paris and the hills of Nancy? It is impossible to be certain. The Germans say that it was the disastrous visit of Colonel Hentsch, the plenipotentiary of Great Headquarters, to Bülow and Kluck at noon on Wednesday September 9th. The French say that it was the march of the French 42nd Division under Foch on the evening of the 8th. It may also be argued that it was the advance of the British 2nd Corps north of the Marne early on the 9th, which by good fortune touched the most sensitive portion of the German front. I think that the right answer is that there was no one such cause; there were half a dozen.

But let us take a moment seven months later—the attack of the British fleet on the Dardanelles. On Thursday, March 18th, Admiral John de Robeck launched his assault on the Narrows. He silenced most of the forts and the attack seemed to be proceeding well, until suddenly he began to lose ships from mines; first the *Bouvet*, then the *Irresistible*, then the *Ocean*. But when he broke off the action he intended to resume it later, and he and the Government in London were still confident that it would be carried presently to a successful issue.

Then something happened to change his view. In the second volume of his book, *The World Crisis*, Mr Winston Churchill has told dramatically the tale of that see-saw of hopes and fears. On the 23rd Admiral de Robeck, after a talk with Sir Ian Hamilton, telegraphed to London that he could not continue the naval attack till the army was ready to co-operate, and that that would not be before April 14th. Lord Fisher promptly swung round to his side, his argument being that we need not lose any more ships when Britain was bound to win in any case, seeing that the British were the lost ten tribes of Israel! The other

Admirals, as Mr Churchill says, "stuck their toes in". Mr Asquith, though inclined to Mr Churchill's view, was not prepared to intervene and over-ride naval opinion both at home and on the spot. The naval attack was dropped, and we waited for a month to land an army, with results which are only too well remembered. Turkey was at her last gasp, and to her amazement was given a breathing space, of which she made brilliant use.

What made Admiral de Robeck change his mind, for it is clear that it was his change of mind which was the determining factor? It may have been his talk with Sir Ian Hamilton which opened to him a prospect of combined operations against the Gallipoli Peninsula, a prospect which he had not realised before, and which relieved him of a share of his heavy responsibilities. But we can narrow down the cause to something still smaller. What made his responsibilities seem so heavy? It was the presence of unsuspected mines in the

Narrows on March 18th that caused our losses and thereby shook the nerve of the naval staff. How did the mines get there? Ten days earlier a little Turkish steamer called the *Nousret* had dodged the British night patrol of destroyers, and laid a new line of twenty mines in Eren Kui Bay. On March 16th three of these mines were destroyed by our sweepers, but we did not realise that they were part of a *line* of mines, and so we did not look for more. If we had made a different deduction there would have been no casualties on the 18th, and de Robeck on the 19th or 20th must have taken his fleet into the Sea of Marmora.

The officer in charge of the little *Nousret* did not know, probably—if he is still alive—does not yet know, the fatefulness of his deed. It altered the whole course of the War, for at that moment Turkey was in the most literal truth at her last gasp. We have the evidence of Enver; we have the evidence of half a dozen Germans on the spot.

She was almost out of munitions, and her resistance in the Narrows that day was the last effort of which she was capable in defence. Her Government had its papers packed, and was about to leave for the uplands of Asia Minor. I have talked to a distinguished German diplomatist who was then in Constantinople, and he has described to me the complete despair of the Turkish Government and their German advisers. They believed that it was mathematically certain that in a day or two Constantinople would be in British hands. When they heard that the British fleet had given up the attack they could not believe their ears; it seemed to them the most insane renunciation of a certain victory.

The occupation of Constantinople would have meant that Turkey fell out of the War. It would have meant much more. Bulgaria would never have become an ally of the Central Powers. The way would have been prepared to supply the needs of Russia, and Russia would have been kept in close touch with her Western allies. There would have been no Russian Revolution, or, if revolution had come, it would have taken a very different form. Austria would have been caught in flank and presently put out of action. It would have meant that in all human likelihood the Allies would have been victorious early in the year 1916. What oceans of blood and treasure would have been saved; what a different world we should be living in to-day, had an obscure Turkish sailorman not laid his mines in the way he did on that March evening!

III

I have put before you a few crucial moments in history, when a great event has been determined by some small thing which it is difficult to describe as anything but an accident—something which we cannot explain by reference to profound causes, something which it is not easy to rationalise.

My argument is a modest one: simply that we should not attempt to impress our modern whim upon the immutable past, and press our theories of historical processes too far. We must have these theories, and they explain a great deal, but they do not explain everything. We must interpret as well as chronicle, we must attempt to show the interconnection of events; but let us be chary about large mechanical principles of interpretation which explain too much. Let us by all means accept the doctrine of predestination, whether in its metaphysical or theological form, so long as we do not try to show in detail how it works. The danger is not with it, for at bottom it is a poetic or religious conception rather than a scientific. The danger is rather with the pseudo-scientists, the Buckles and Guizots and Taines and their modern counterparts, who dogmatise about the details, and believe that they can provide a neat explanation of everything in the past by subsuming it under a dozen categories; and with the doctrinaires, like Marx and his school, who would fit the centuries into the iron bed of a single formula. The answer is an appeal to facts, to the stubborn nodules of the unrelated and the inexplicable which everywhere confront us. The romantic accident cannot be expelled by the mechanical doctrine. It will still come out of the void, alter the course of history, and disappear before it can be classified.

This parlour game, which I suggest to you for a winter fireside, has its own seriousness. To reflect how easily the course of things might have been different is to learn perspective and humility. The world is bigger and more intricate than we thought, and there are more things in heaven and earth than we can bring within the pale of any copy-book philosophy. To-day, physical science is in a modest mood. It admits frankly a large hinterland of mystery. "While Newton", David Hume wrote in his *Dialogues*, "seemed to draw off the veil from the mystery of Nature, he showed at the same time the imperfections of the mechanical philosophy; and thereby restored her ultimate secrets to that obscurity in which they ever did, and ever will, remain." The physical scientist of to-day, though he may not approve the scepticism of Hume's last sentence, is well aware of the imperfections of a mechanical creed. Philosophy, too, has, I think, learned humility. At any rate she has abated something of her exclusive arrogance, and the lines of Pope have almost become true:

> Physic of Metaphysic begs defence,
> And Metaphysic calls for aid on Sense.

Surely the Muse of History, whose domain has not the rigour of the natural sciences, or the ancient right of metaphysics to dogmatise, should not be behind her sisters in this noble modesty. I suggest as a suitable motto for Clio's servants some words of one of the greatest of them, a passage of Burke in his *Letters on a Regicide Peace*:

It is often impossible, in these political en-quiries, to find any proportion between the apparent force of any moral causes we may assign, and their known operation. We are therefore obliged to deliver up that operation to mere chance; or, more piously (perhaps more rationally), to the occasional interposition and the irresistible hand of the Great Disposer.

www.ingramcontent.com/pod-product-compliance
Ingram Content Group UK Ltd.
Pitfield, Milton Keynes, MK11 3LW, UK
UKHW042141280225
455719UK00001B/10